ARTHUR MITCHELL

ARTHUR MITCHELL

by Tobi Tobias

illustrated by Carole Byard

Thomas Y. Crowell Company
New York

Library of Congress Cataloging in Publication Data. Tobias, Tobi. Arthur Mitchell. SUMMARY: A biography of the black ballet dancer who gave up his career as a star with the New York City Ballet to found the Dance Theatre of Harlem. 1. Mitchell, Arthur, 1934–   —Juv. lit. 2. Ballet—Juv. lit. 3. Dance Theatre of Harlem—Juv. lit. [1. Mitchell, Arthur, 1934–   2. Dancers. 3. Negroes—Biography. 4. Dance Theatre of Harlem] I. Byard, Carole M., illus. II. Title. GV1785.M53T62   792.8′092′4 [B] [92] 74-13730 ISBN 0-690-00661-6. ISBN 0-690-00662-4 (LB).

1   2   3   4   5   6   7   8   9   10

ARTHUR MITCHELL

A CROWELL
BIOGRAPHY

Whenever company came to Arthur Mitchell's house, the young boy ran behind a curtain and called, "Watch me, everyone." Then he'd come out dancing and singing. "Arthur, you stop showing off," his mother warned, even though she was proud of the lively, happy way he moved. It made her feel good just to look at him. Everybody else laughed and clapped. "You watch that boy," they said. "He'll be a dancer one day."

At the beginning, though, there wasn't much dancing in Arthur's life. In fact there wasn't much of anything except hard work—and the warmth and love of a close-knit family. Arthur was born on March 27, 1934, in Harlem, a large black community in New York City. Like many people in the neighborhood, Arthur's parents were poor, even though both of them were working as hard as they could.

I

Arthur's mother, Willie Mae Mitchell, kept house and took care of her large family. There was a new baby every year. After Arthur came Charles, Laura, Herbert, and Shirley. To get a little extra money, Mrs. Mitchell minded other people's children, along with her own.

Arthur's father, Arthur Mitchell, Senior, had a knack for doing anything he set his hand to—carpentry, plumbing, electrical repairs. He used all his skills, and plain hard labor, as superintendent of the apartment house where the family lived. His pay was low, but the job gave them their few small rooms rent-free.

Arthur's father expected his boys to help him with the heavy chores. They stoked coal for the furnace, swept the sidewalk, shoveled the snow in winter, and hauled huge bundles of trash away. When they finished, they were filthy and exhausted. Arthur hated it. He also hated the fact that his father had hardly any time to have fun with him. Sometimes it seemed the only thing they did together was work.

But soon Arthur figured something out. If a job had to be done, it didn't do him any good to be sad or angry about it. So he turned it into what he liked best—a performance. He danced his way through the work instead of walking, and cracked jokes to his brothers and sisters, making them double over with laughter. He got his work done fast and he made it look like fun. No matter what Arthur had to do, he made sure people found him smiling.

The best times in the Mitchell household were Sunday mornings. Arthur's father got up early and cooked—crisp fried chicken or juicy pork chops and cornmeal pancakes. Delicious smells filled the crowded apartment. Everyone sat around the kitchen table, talking and laughing together. Those were the times Arthur could really feel the love in his family.

Then Mrs. Mitchell and her children went off to church. Mr. Mitchell refused to go with them. He said all the preachers were crooks. It was difficult for him to believe in the goodness they talked about when he had such a hard life. All he knew was a load of bitter, backbreaking work and bad times, and no chance that he could see of any change. But for Arthur's mother and many of her friends, the church was the center of the neighborhood. There they came together and shared their thoughts, their troubles, their plans and hopes and dreams. Arthur sang in the choir with people he had known all his life.

He went to school in the same community. Learning was easy for him and he enjoyed it. He made many friends. People liked him because he was lively, gay, and full of new ideas. He was the leader of any group he joined. He also spent some time by himself every day, reading and thinking.

During these quiet hours Arthur realized that he wanted something more than what he and the people close to him had now. Better food, better clothes, better things to do, a better way of living. He knew he'd have to work for these things, and he was willing to work. He was used to it. Arthur Mitchell was sure he could do whatever had to be done to get ahead.

He had a job of his own as soon as he was old enough to carry a shoeshine box. He ran errands for people in the neighborhood who gave him a nickel or a dime. He washed windows. He worked as a delivery boy. Later he had a newspaper route.

One cold, dark, winter afternoon, as he was coming home from his route, a gang of white boys suddenly appeared at the end of the street. "There's a nigger!" they yelled. They jumped on Arthur and beat him up, cutting his face with a switchblade. For the first time, Arthur realized that being black could hurt

him. The next afternoon, though, he was back on his route, determined that no one was going to stop him from what he wanted to do.

At home, there were other problems. For a long time Mr. Mitchell had been angry and unhappy because he couldn't care for his family the way he wanted to. He started to drink, and for a while the whiskey would help him forget his troubles. But it made him drunk and sick, and then he couldn't work at all. When he did make some money, he'd buy fancy clothes and presents, instead of the food the family needed. His wife would scream and cry, but it did no good.

After he acted this way, he felt terrible. Often he felt so bad, he thought he would never straighten his life out. Finally he just couldn't face the people he loved, and he ran away. Now the family had to manage on its own.

8

Arthur worked every day after school and on the weekends. He tried to take the place of a father for his younger brothers and sisters. It was a heavy load for a boy of thirteen.

Still, there was room for good times. One night, at a junior high school party, his teacher saw him dancing. It wasn't just Arthur's feet that were dancing, but his eyes and his smile and every muscle in his body. It was as good as any performance she had ever seen on the stage.

She told Arthur he ought to go to the High School of Performing Arts, a special school for young people with talent for dancing and acting. He would have to prove his talent by showing a group of judges what he could do. Many of the students trying out would be able to show off years of dancing and acting lessons. Arthur had never had the chance for this kind of training.

The next summer he went to an old man who was once in show business. From him, Arthur learned an old-time song-and-dance act. He went to the tryouts in a fancy, rented evening suit and a tall top hat. There he performed his easy-moving, soft-shoe routine to the tune of "Steppin' Out With My Baby." The judges were astonished, but delighted. The other students showed them the complicated kinds of dancing they expected to see. Arthur moved simply, with his own proud

energy, rhythm and happiness all over his
body.

Arthur was accepted at Performing Arts,
but his first year there was very hard. The
school taught two forms of dance. One was
classical ballet, an old, beautiful, and difficult
form of movement. Arthur studied modern
dance, which broke away from the set patterns
of ballet and moved in new, freer ways. All of
the young dancers spent hours every day doing
exercises to train their bodies.

For Arthur, the dance classes were nearly impossible. He had a natural gift for performing, but his body was stiff and tight. He pulled and pushed and sweated, trying to make it do what he wanted it to do.

Finally the head of the school said he'd never become a dancer and told him he'd better try something else. That made Arthur furious. He ran off to class and tried so hard to stretch his stubborn body that he tore several muscles. The pain was terrible, but Arthur's mind was made up. No matter what it took, he was going to be a dancer. From then on, he began to improve.

Whenever people asked Arthur to perform, he would dance, even if they couldn't pay him. He wanted the experience of working in the theater, and he loved dancing. But many times, when he tried out for a role in a show, he didn't get it, although he was the best

dancer there. He saw that the good parts went to white dancers. He couldn't understand why, and it hurt him. He promised himself he was going to make some changes.

When he was eighteen, Arthur graduated from Performing Arts. He won the school's highest dance award and a scholarship to go on with his training in modern dance at Bennington College. But a man named Lincoln Kirstein offered him an even better opportunity. Kirstein had created the world-famous New York City Ballet with George Balanchine, a choreographer who made amazingly beautiful and unusual ballets. Now Kirstein was inviting Arthur to study classical dance at the company's training academy, the School of American Ballet.

In 1952 there were not many black people in ballet. It was still a white man's art. In his blunt, honest way, Kirstein told Arthur that a black dancer would have to be twice as good as a white one to succeed. White audiences were used to seeing white dancers in ballet. They wouldn't be interested in watching Arthur Mitchell perform unless he could offer them something special. It wasn't fair, and it didn't make sense, but it was true.

This was just the kind of challenge Arthur liked. He believed he had special qualities as a black dancer—a sense of style and rhythm and freedom, an ability to make his body express something when he moved. Now he saw a chance to combine those talents with the strict technique and the elegance of a classical dancer. If he could put those things together, Arthur thought, there would be no performer like him. He'd be so different and so good that when he tried out for a part, they'd *have* to take him. His answer to Kirstein was "Yes."

For the next three years, Arthur's routine

was the same, day in and day out. He got up early to do two hours of exercises by himself, just to prepare his body for class. He took three ballet classes a day, using every ounce of power and concentration he had. In addition to his regular lessons, he studied with the fine ballet teacher Karel Shook, who became his close friend. The only time Arthur wasn't dancing was when he was eating, sleeping, or working to support his family.

Ballet training was long, hard, often discouraging, but tremendously exciting. Most of the time, Arthur's muscles were aching with strain. He was always dripping with sweat, constantly fighting his own tiredness. But for a few minutes each day, as he stretched and leaped and jumped and turned, he felt like the king of his own body, a prince of space. Dancing might be one of the hardest careers in the world, but he couldn't imagine doing anything else.

Still he wondered—bitterly sometimes—if a black dancer could ever succeed in an important American ballet company. He thought perhaps he should go back to modern dance, where black talent was welcome. Night after night, he sat in the theater, watching white dancers perform Balanchine's vivid, brilliant ballets. He knew this was the kind of dancing he wanted to do. "Don't be a fool," his friends said. "They'll never take you." Just when Arthur was ready to give up hoping, he was asked to join the New York City Ballet.

His first performance with them was on November 8, 1955. He danced a leading role as a cowboy in George Balanchine's *Western Symphony.* When Arthur came out on stage, he heard a woman in the audience gasp. "Look," she said, "they've got a nigger in the company."

Arthur went on dancing. He wasn't going to let any person's cruel foolishness stop him. The steps he had to do were fast and complicated, but he made them look easy. "You know," he heard the same voice say, "he's good." Arthur knew he was good. He was glad this thoughtless woman was finding it out. That night, and in the ten years that followed, Arthur proved that a black dancer should be judged by his dancing, nothing else.

After years of training, his body was strong. He could make it move almost any way he wanted to. He used every inch of his body when he danced, so that each movement seemed important and interesting. Smiling, and sure of himself, he made everything he did look right, even when he made a mistake, or fell down, as he often did in his first year with

the company. Arthur let the audience see how much he enjoyed dancing, and they enjoyed it with him.

Slowly, he was given parts in many different kinds of ballets. Some of them told a story. Here Arthur showed his talent for acting. Some of them were simply fascinating movement to music. Some of the ballets were serious. Some were pure fun. Each one was a chance for Arthur to learn something new.

The greatest honor came when a role in a ballet was made especially for him. In 1957 Balanchine created *Agon*. The strange, beautiful movement of this ballet, with its odd rhythms, was different from anything that had been done before. Arthur danced a leading role.

In 1962, when Balanchine staged *A Midsummer Night's Dream*, he gave Arthur the part of Puck, the mischievous, magic-making elf. The role was perfect for the swift movement of

Arthur's dancing and his gift for making people laugh. Later, others danced this part, but no one ever danced it better.

Arthur became a top star in the New York City Ballet. But he was still the only black dancer in the company. He realized it was not enough to make his own success in the world. He wanted to help other black people.

Arthur Mitchell's new work began in the spring of 1968, with his idea for an all-black classical ballet company. It would have a school for training its own dancers. Many people said blacks were not suited to classical dancing. They said the shape of black people's bodies and the way they moved wasn't right for ballet's long, smooth, flowing lines. These lies kept most black dancers out of ballet for years and years. But Arthur believed that a black man or woman with talent, a strong desire to succeed, and the will to work could become anything he or she wanted to be. What black people needed was the chance to try.

Arthur and his old friend Karel Shook started in an empty Harlem garage with thirty students and four professional dancers. Classes were given morning, afternoon, and night. They were trying to train dancers faster than anyone had ever done before.

"Now!" Arthur would shout at the students as they worked harder and harder. "We've got to do it now. We haven't got years and years. Faster!" he yelled as they went spinning across the floor, cutting through the

24

air. "Stronger! Clearer! You know you're beautiful. Now *show me* you're beautiful."

Arthur's energy and faith and drive to succeed spread like a fire through his young dancers. They improved more quickly than anyone believed was possible. Arthur began to make short ballets for them. He used a platform built in the garage for a stage.

People in the neighborhood stopped to watch through the open doors. They were fascinated by the strength and beauty of the dancing. Everyone wanted to share in what was happening. The young people asked, "Can we join?" They joined and they danced. Older people sewed costumes, brought food, and offered what little money they had to buy dancing shoes and practice clothes. Black dancers from all over the country heard about Arthur's project and wanted to be part of it. By the end of the summer, there were four hundred students. A small group of them were ready to perform for the public. It was the beginning of a professional company—the Dance Theatre of Harlem.

In the fall, they moved to a larger space in a neighborhood church. Here Arthur developed the school he had dreamed of. It taught many forms of dance: ballet, modern, tap dancing, jazz, and the native dances of Africa and the Caribbean islands. Arthur wanted his dancers to be prepared to move in many different ways. Music was taught, and the sounds of pianos, guitars, and drums filled the old church. As students learned to sew, they designed and made costumes for the company.

There were acting lessons and training in lighting and carpentry for the stage.

Anyone was welcome in the school—white, black, young, old, talented or not, even if he could only pay a few cents for the lessons. As long as a student wanted to learn, there was a place for him.

The best of the young dancers were chosen for the company, which was growing quickly. Now Arthur was able to make more difficult and interesting ballets for them. He liked to use African dance. Its powerful, rhythmic movements were made close to the ground, to the beat of drums. He combined this with ballet's smooth classical steps and airy lifts, to make a special style for the Dance Theatre of Harlem. Other fine choreographers—white and black—came to work with these eager, gifted dancers.

Still the Dance Theatre of Harlem was facing a big problem. It takes thousands of dollars to pay for the dancers, musicians, and teachers, the lighting, scenery, and costumes that a ballet company must have. Where was this money going to come from?

Arthur never brooded over difficulties, but immediately started figuring out what to do. He went to the rich business organizations. Through his strength and hope, and the fine work already done, he convinced them to support the Dance Theatre of Harlem. The Ford Foundation said they would give half the money needed if the dancers could earn the other half.

To do this, the company went out on tour.

They traveled, by bus, from place to place, to perform. They went to small towns and big cities. They danced in schools, in community meeting houses, on rickety platforms, and in splendid, large theaters. Each time, in a different place, they explained the work a dancer must do in the classroom. Then they performed ballets to show what can be done on the stage.

Sometimes the people watching them had never seen ballet dancing before. Then there were performances for people who had seen some of the best dancing in the world. The Dance Theatre of Harlem was a huge success at the Jacob's Pillow Dance Festival in Massachusetts and at the Guggenheim Museum in its first big performance in New York City. The company also went to the Caribbean islands and then to Europe. Audiences everywhere loved these lively, handsome dancers.

All this time, the school and the company were getting larger and doing more work. By 1971 they had outgrown their space in the church. Still, they wanted to stay in the community. The company might travel very far, but they would always come home to Harlem, where their roots were.

Finally they found an old warehouse near the street on which Arthur grew up. It was run-down, but large and filled with light. With their performing, the dancers raised enough money to change the junk-filled warehouse into rooms fitted out for work in dancing, music, sewing, and stagecraft. In 1971 the

Dance Theatre of Harlem moved into its new home.

There is never any end to the group's work. It keeps growing. On April 16, 1974, the company gave the opening performance of their first long New York season. It was a triumph. At the end, as the dancers bowed, the audience rose to its feet, clapping hard and loud, and shouting praises to them. But early the next morning the company was back in the practice room, trying to do better.

Arthur is always at the center of this work that never stops. He knows he must do more than anyone else. He is teacher, choreographer, director, manager, businessman, and often like a father to the children of the school and the young people in the company. He does not perform now. There is no time. He has given up his own dancing career to help hundreds of other people dance.

There is almost no room in Arthur's life for anything outside the Dance Theatre of Harlem, although he loves people and has many interests. He has deep friendships with all kinds of people: white and black, men and women, old and young. He is close to his family and the people in the neighborhood where he grew up. But the work comes first. Through it, he is helping other people, giving them joy, a purpose in life, and a chance for success.

"I am a fighter," Arthur Mitchell says, "and I fight with my art."

32

ABOUT THE AUTHOR

Tobi Tobias is a Contributing Editor of *Dance Magazine* and one of the gifted young critics writing for an ever-growing dance audience in this country. She also takes great pleasure in writing both fiction and nonfiction for young people. Among her recent books for children is ISAMU NOGUCHI: THE LIFE OF A SCULPTOR, published by Thomas Y. Crowell Company.

Ms. Tobias lives with her husband and their two children in the brownstone they are renovating on New York's Upper West Side.

ABOUT THE ILLUSTRATOR

Carole Byard is a talented young artist who has illustrated several picture books, and whose spirited drawings of dancers performing have appeared in magazines. Ms. Byard was born and grew up in Atlantic City. Since studying at the New York Phoenix School of Design, she has lived in New York City.